Readers
LEVEL **2**

Looking After Me

How Do We Move?

Sally Morgan

Quarto
Library

This library edition published in 2015 by Quarto Library.,
an imprint of Quarto Publishing Group USA Inc.
3 Wrigley, Suite A
Irvine, CA 92618

© 2015 QEB Publishing, Published by Quarto Library.,
an imprint of Quarto Publishing Group USA Inc.

Distributed in the United States and Canada by
Lerner Publisher Services
241 First Avenue North
Minneapolis, MN 55401 U.S.A.
www.lernerbooks.com

A CIP record for this book is available from the Library of Congress.

ISBN 978 1 93958 184 6

Printed in China

Picture credits

(t = top, b = bottom, l = left, r = right, c = center, fc = front cover)

Shutterstock fc Sergey Novikov, 4-5 Pressmaster, 5tr wavebreakmedia,
7b Feng Yu, 11 Dimitri Iundt, 12 Patrik Giardino, 13 SergiyN,
14br Andrey_Kuzmin, 15c bikeriderlondon, 16c Don Mason,
17 Owen Franken, 18-19 Luis Louro, 19br Golden Pixels LLC,
20-21 l i g h t p o e t, 21t Anton Balazh, 22-23 lapetitelumiere

Words in **bold** can be found in the Glossary on page 24.

Contents

Moving Around

We can all move
in different ways.
We use our legs
to walk and run.
We can wave
our arms.

We hop and skip,
jump and climb.
We can swim in
water, too.

How many
other ways
can you move?

5

Your Skeleton

There are bones inside your body. They make up your **skeleton**.

There are long bones in your arms and legs.

Can you feel the bones in your arms?

There are short bones
in your hands and feet.

Can you feel the bones
in your feet?

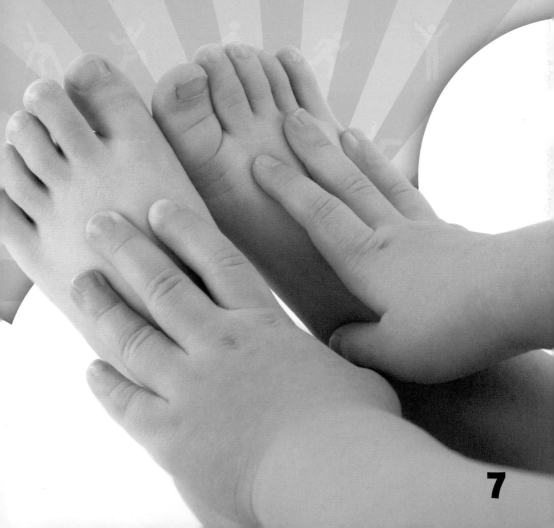

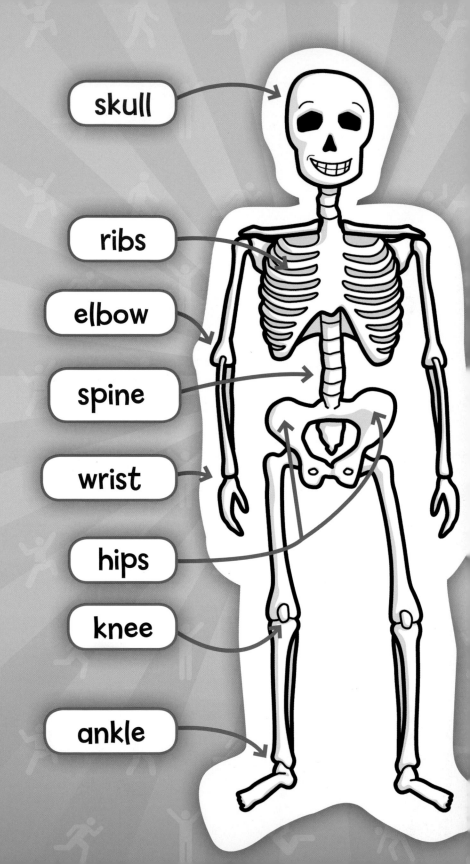

skull

ribs

elbow

spine

wrist

hips

knee

ankle

8

Your skeleton is made up of lots of different bones.

Your skeleton **supports** and **protects** your body.

Without a skeleton, your body would be floppy like jello.

Muscles

Your bones can't move on their own. They are moved by **muscles**. Your muscles are attached to your bones.

Muscles move bones by pulling on them. A muscle pulls by getting shorter and fatter.

biceps

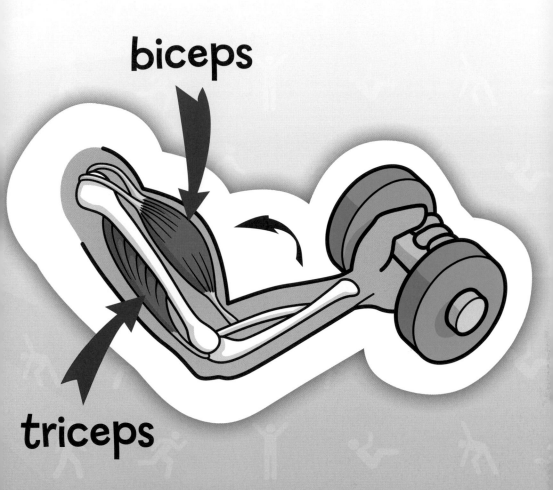

triceps

Two muscles help you move your arm. The muscle that bends your arm is the biceps. The triceps makes your arm straight.

Put your hand around
the top part of your arm.
Now bend your elbow.

Can you feel the muscles
moving under your skin?

Athletes spend many hours training. Training helps build up their muscles.

Walking and Running

When you walk, you lift one leg off the ground, move it forward, and put it down. Then you move the other leg.

You always have one foot on the ground when you are walking.

When you run, both of your feet can be off the ground at the same time.

Climbing

People can climb walls and trees, and even cliffs and mountains.

This climber is using his hands and feet to climb a mountain.

16

This girl is learning to climb on a special rock climbing wall.

To climb, you grip with your hands. Then you move your body up by pulling with your arms and pushing with your legs.

Jumping and Hopping

When you jump, you push your body off the ground using your legs.

If you run and then jump, you can can leap even farther.

Hopping is jumping up and down on one leg.

Can you hop?

Swimming

You use your arms and legs to move through the water when you swim.

Pull the water back with your arms, and kick with your feet to push forward.

To dive and swim underwater you have to hold your breath. You can't breathe underwater.

22

Do you like to swim?

Glossary

athlete someone who is very good at sports like running and jumping

muscles the fleshy parts of your body that move the bones

protect to keep something safe

skeleton the bony framework of a person or animal

support to hold something so that it doesn't fall down

ma   7-16